A Beginning-to-Read Book

A New Baby

by Mary Lindeen

NORWOOD HOUSE PRESS

DEAR CAREGIVER, The *Beginning to Read—Read and Discover* books provide emergent readers the opportunity to explore the world through nonfiction while building early reading skills. The text integrates both common sight words and content vocabulary. These key words are featured on lists provided at the back of the book to help your child expand his or her sight word recognition, which helps build reading fluency. The content words expand vocabulary and support comprehension.

Nonfiction text is any text that is factual. The Common Core State Standards call for an increase in the amount of informational text reading among students. The Standards aim to promote college and career readiness among students. Preparation for college and career endeavors requires proficiency in reading complex informational texts in a variety of content areas. You can help your child build a foundation by introducing nonfiction early. To further support the CCSS, you will find Reading Reinforcement activities at the back of the book that are aligned to these Standards.

Above all, the most important part of the reading experience is to have fun and enjoy it!

Sincerely,

Shannon Cannon, Ph.D.
Literacy Consultant

Norwood House Press
For more information about Norwood House Press please visit our website at
www.norwoodhousepress.com or call 866-565-2900.
© 2022 Norwood House Press. Beginning-to-Read™ is a trademark of Norwood House Press.
All rights reserved. No part of this book may be reproduced or utilized in any form or by any
means without written permission from the publisher.

Editor: Judy Kentor Schmauss
Designer: Sara Radka

Photo Credits:
All images sourced from Getty Images.

Library of Congress Cataloging-in-Publication Data
Names: Lindeen, Mary, author.
Title: A new baby / by Mary Lindeen.
Description: Chicago : Norwood House Press, 2022. | Series: A beginning-to-read book | Audience: Grades K-1
| Summary: "Describes what it means to have a new baby at home, including what babies need, what babies
do, and how to care for them. This title includes a note to caregivers, reading activities, and a word list. An
early social and emotional book that includes reading activities and a word list"– Provided by publisher.
Identifiers: LCCN 2021049735 (print) | LCCN 2021049736 (ebook) | ISBN 9781684507894
(hardcover) | ISBN 9781684047338 (paperback) | ISBN 9781684047376 (epub)
Subjects: LCSH: Infants–Juvenile literature.
Classification: LCC HQ774 .L54 2022 (print) | LCC HQ774 (ebook) | DDC 305.232–dc23/eng/20211108
LC record available at https://lccn.loc.gov/2021049735
LC ebook record available at https://lccn.loc.gov/2021049736

Hardcover ISBN: 978-1-68450-789-4
Paperback ISBN: 978-1-68404-733-8

347N—012022
Manufactured in the United States of America in North Mankato, Minnesota.

Shh . . .

The new baby is sleeping.

Babies need
lots of sleep.

Sleep helps
babies grow.

A new baby needs blankets, too.

A blanket helps a baby
feel safe and warm.

All babies need food.

But new babies don't have teeth yet.

They drink their food.

Babies also
need baths.

A small bathtub
is just the
right size.

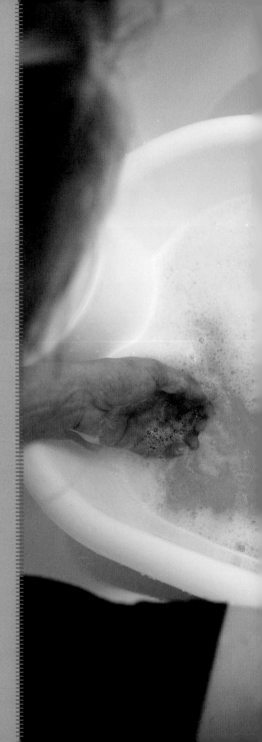

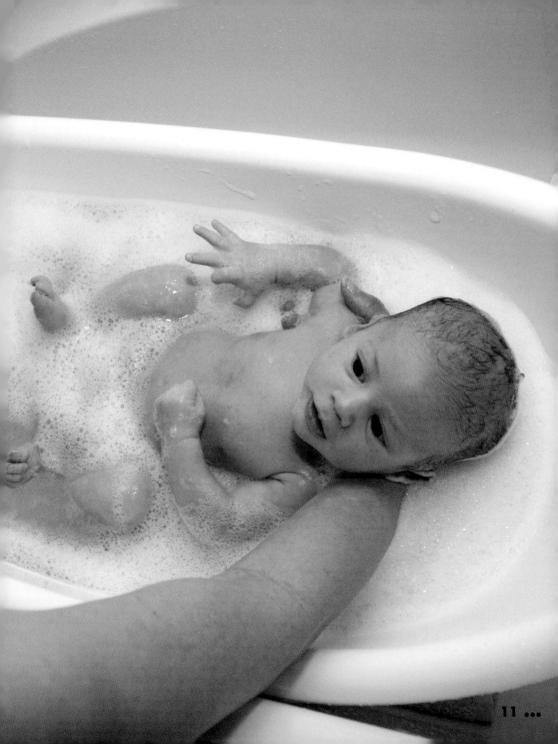

Babies need toys, too.

New babies can't hold toys.

But they like to look at colorful things.

A new baby also needs to be carried.

People can carry babies in their arms.

And they can use baby carriers like this one.

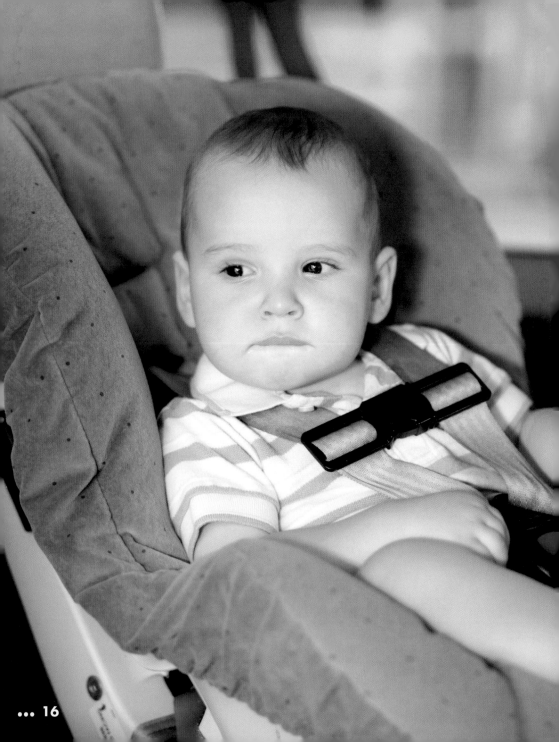

Sometimes,
babies need to
ride in cars.

A special seat
keeps the baby
safe in the car.

A stroller
gives a baby
another safe place
to ride.

Babies also
need help with
their feelings.

Babies cry
when they feel
sad or mad.

Gently rocking or patting a baby can help him feel better.

Then he will stop crying.

Softly talking or
singing to a baby
can help, too.

A new baby
needs a lot
of help . . .

. . . and a lot
of love!

...READING REINFORCEMENT...

CRAFT AND STRUCTURE

To check your child's understanding of the organization of the book, recreate the following chart on a sheet of paper. Ask your child to complete the chart by writing what a baby needs in the web:

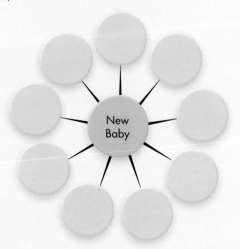

New Baby

VOCABULARY: Learning Content Words

Content words are words that are specific to a particular topic. All the content words in this book can be found on page 32. Use some or all of these content words to complete one or more of the following activities:

1. Help your child make up sentences that use two or more of the words.

2. Help your child cut out pictures from magazines that help them remember the words.

3. Do a word hunt around your home for the words.

4. Give your child several clues to the meaning of the words and have them guess the word.

5. Write the words on slips of paper and put them in a bowl. Have your child pick a slip of paper, define the word on it, and find the word in the book.

FOUNDATIONAL SKILLS: Plural Nouns

Nouns name a person, place, or thing. A singular noun means one. A plural noun means more than one. Have your child identify the plural nouns in the list below. Then help your child find plural nouns in this book.

dog	flowers	sofa
kittens	rocks	tables

CLOSE READING OF INFORMATIONAL TEXT

Close reading helps children comprehend text. It includes reading a text, discussing it with others, and answering questions about it. Use these questions to discuss this book with your child:

1. What do you think is the most important thing a baby needs? Why?

2. Why do babies need help with their feelings?

3. Why do you think babies cry?

4. What is one way to help take care of a baby?

5. How is a baby the same as you? Different?

6. Do you think taking care of a baby is hard? Why or why not?

FLUENCY

Fluency is the ability to read accurately with speed and expression. Help your child practice fluency by using one or more of the following activities:

1. Reread the book to your child at least two times while he or she uses a finger to track each word as it is read.

2. Read a line of the book, then reread it as your child reads along with you.

3. Ask your child to go back through the book and read the words he or she knows.

4. Have your child practice reading the book several times to improve accuracy, rate, and expression.

··· Word List ···

A New Baby uses the 86 words listed below. *High-frequency words* are those words that are used most often in the English language. They are sometimes referred to as *sight words* because children need to learn to recognize them automatically when they read. *Content words* are any words specific to a particular topic. Regular practice reading these words will enhance your child's ability to read with greater fluency and comprehension.

High-Frequency Words

a	can	just	place	this
all	give(s)	like	right	to
also	have	look	small	too
and	he	new	the	use
another	help(s)	of	their	when
at	him	one	then	will
be	in	or	they	with
but	is	people	things	

Content Words

arms	carriers	grow	sad	stop
babies	carry	hold	safe	stroller
baby	cars	keeps	seat	talking
baths	colorful	lot(s)	shhhh	teeth
bathtub	cry(ing)	love	singing	toys
better	don't	mad	size	warm
blanket(s)	drink	need(s)	sleep(ing)	yet
can't	feel(ings)	patting	softly	
car	food	ride	sometimes	
carried	gently	rocking	special	

••• About the Author

Mary Lindeen is a writer, editor, parent, and former elementary school teacher. She has written more than 100 books for children and edited many more. She specializes in early literacy instruction and books for young readers, especially nonfiction.